The Longest Tunnels

Susan K. Mitchell
AR B.L.: 5.8
Points: 1.0   MG

MEGASTRUCTURES

THE LONGEST TUNNELS

by Susan K. Mitchell

Gareth Stevens
Publishing

Please visit our web site at: **www.garethstevens.com**
For a free color catalog describing Gareth Stevens Publishing's
list of high-quality books, call 1-800-542-2595 (USA)
or 1-800-387-3178 (Canada).

Library of Congress Cataloging-in-Publication Data

Mitchell, Susan K.
    The longest tunnels / by Susan K. Mitchell.
      p. cm. — (Megastructures)
    Includes bibliographical references and index.
    ISBN-10: 0-8368-8365-9 (lib. bdg.)
    ISBN-13: 978-0-8368-8365-7 (lib. bdg.)
    1. Tunnels—Juvenile literature. I. Title.
  TA805.M58   2007
  624.1'93—dc22   2007008344

This edition first published in 2008 by
Gareth Stevens Publishing
A Weekly Reader® Company
1 Reader's Digest Road
Pleasantville, NY 10570-7000 USA

Editorial direction: Mark J. Sachner
Editor: Barbara Kiely Miller
Art direction and design: Tammy West
Picture research: Diane Laska-Swanke
Production: Jessica Yanke
Illustrations: Spectrum Creative Inc.

Picture credits: Cover, title © Najlah Feanny/CORBIS; pp. 5, 10, 12, 26-27, 29 © AP Images; p. 7 © Wolfgang Kaehler/CORBIS; p. 8 © Hulton-Deutsch Collection/CORBIS; p. 16 © Eric K. K. Yu/CORBIS; p. 17 © Bill Ross/CORBIS; pp. 20-21 © Bettmann/CORBIS; p. 25 © Edward Rozzo/CORBIS

Printed in the United States of America

1 2 3 4 5 6 7 8 9 11 10 09 08 07

CONTENTS

On the Cover: New York's Holland Tunnel runs underneath the Hudson River. More than thirty-three million drivers pass through it each year.

CHAPTER 1

DIGGING DEEP

Not much can stop a tunnel from being built. Tunnels can pass through mountains. They can reach deep under water. A maze of tunnels can even lie under crowded city streets. Before tunnels were constructed, travelers had to find a way around or over obstacles in their paths. But these detours could make for much longer trips. Today, tunnels give travelers ways to move right through those obstacles. One of the main reasons that people build tunnels is to make transportation easier.

In many places, mountains are steep and snowy. Driving over them on narrow mountain roads is far too dangerous for most people. The only way to cross some seas or rivers is a choppy ferry ride. This kind of travel can also be very dangerous. To provide safer, shorter routes over places like these, engineers build tunnels.

Sometimes, engineers build tunnels because city streets are crowded. Too many cars bring travel to a slow

MEGA FACTS

Tunnels have been used during times of war. Soldiers dug tunnels to hide in or to travel without being seen. Sometimes, the soldiers lived in the tunnels for years. The most famous war tunnels are the Cu Chi Tunnels used by North Vietnamese soldiers during the Vietnam War.

crawl. Tunnels built for underground subways and trains help people quickly get from place to place.

Some tunnels, however, do not help with transportation at all. Engineers design these tunnels to carry water, gas, or electricity to buildings and other places. Other tunnels are constructed in mines. They provide a way for workers to gather coal, minerals, or gems from deep under the ground.

Dirty Work

The basic design of a tunnel seems fairly simple. It looks like just a long hole. Getting that hole dug, however, is not easy. A geologist, or rock scientist, helps engineers

Today many tunnels are no longer dark, dank places. This tunnel in China is decorated with artifical lighting and plants.

More than Mole Holes

Tunnels are divided into four main categories, based on how and where they are built. Rock tunnels are carved or dug out of solid rock. They are usually built through mountains or under city streets.

Soft-ground tunnels are built under waterways. Engineers and workers have a difficult task. They must figure out ways to support the soggy ground beneath a body of water while digging the tunnel. Sunken tube tunnels can also be used underwater. These tunnels are not dug at all. Large steel tubes are lowered onto the floor of a river or sea. Then divers weld the tubes together.

Cut-and-cover tunnels are different from the other three types of tunnels. To build a cut-and-cover tunnel, workers dig a deep trench, or ditch, into the soil or rocky ground. They then cover the top of the trench with a brick, stone, or concrete roof. The roof allows vehicles to drive over the top of the tunnel.

learn what kinds of rocks the tunnel will have to go through. Different kinds of rocks present different problems. Digging through hard rock is a slow and difficult job. If the rock is too soft, however, a tunnel can collapse. With underwater tunnels, flooding is a risk. Engineers have many things to consider when designing a tunnel.

The earliest tunnels were dug by hand. Workers used hand tools to chip away at solid rock. It was a dangerous job, and people often died. By the 1800s, however, people had new ways to tunnel. Explosives such as gunpowder and dynamite had been discovered. They let workers blast through solid rock much quicker than digging by hand. Workers also began to use mechanical drills instead of hammers and chisels to chip away rock.

One of the biggest advances for tunneling under a waterway was the invention of the tunneling shield. In 1825, French engineer Marc Brunel invented a giant cast-iron frame more than 20 feet (6 m) high. He used it for the first time during the construction of the Thames River Tunnel in England. The tunneling shield provided a temporary support for the Thames Tunnel's soggy walls. It kept the tunnel from caving in on workers.

The tunneling shield was an enormous iron box. It was split into thirty-six separate cells, or sections. The cells were arranged in three levels from top to bottom and twelve rows from side to side, filling the entire space of the tunnel. Each cell was large enough to hold one worker. Boards covered and held back the dirt at the front of the shield's cells. Each worker removed the boards in his cell one at a time. He dug out a couple of inches (centimeters) of the soft earth that was behind the

Many of the military tunnels in Vietnam were only large enough for a person to craw through.

board. Then he secured the board back in place before moving on to the next one. After all the workers had dug behind each board, the entire shield was pushed forward. Although it was a slow method, a tunneling shield made tunneling in the soft, wet ground below a waterway possible.

Behind the men digging the tunnel were even more tunnel workers. Some of these workers removed dirt and other debris, or waste, by various methods. Others lined the freshly dug tunnel with bricks while the tunneling shield supported the earth around them. Today, tunnels are usually lined with sections of concrete or steel that are constructed outside the tunnel and joined together inside.

Since the development of the tunneling shield, there have been many other advances in tunneling construction. New drilling machines and new explosives have made tunneling much safer. Even with these advances, however, tunnels are still some of the longest and most expensive engineering projects in the world.

Although the Thames Tunnel is famous, many other tunnels run under the Thames River. The Dartford-Purfleet Tunnel (*below*) is one of them.

CHAPTER 2

MOVING THROUGH MOUNTAINS

The longest road tunnel in the world is the 15-mile- (24-kilometer-) long Laerdal Tunnel in Norway. It connects the cities of Aurland and Laerdal. Norway is a country full of mountains, and hundreds of tunnels pass through them.

Cold weather and heavy snows in Norway make travel on its mountain roads almost impossible during winter. A tunnel is often the safest way for cars to get from one city to another. The Laerdal Tunnel passes through mountains that reach more than 5,900 feet (1,798 m) high. Because of snow, the roads on the mountain are only open for a few months during summer.

Having a Blast

On March 15, 1995, workers began drilling the Laerdal Tunnel. The tunnel runs deep inside the mountains. Workers used a drill and blast method to dig the tunnel. Huge machines called drilling jumbos did most of the work. Each drilling jumbo had three hydraulic drills

MEGA FACTS

In Norway, mountain regions are called fjells, and bays along the seacoast are called fjords. The mountain region between Aurland and Laerdal is called Filefjell.

attached to it. Workers above the ground controlled the drills by computer.

After the jumbos drilled the holes, workers were able to blast their way through the rock. The jumbos drilled one hundred holes for each blast. Then workers pumped an explosive into the holes. When the workers and the jumbos had moved a safe distance from the blast site, the explosives were detonated, or set off. More than 5,000 blasts were needed to tunnel through the mountain.

An access tunnel was also drilled into the mountain from a side valley. This tunnel was 1 mile (1.6 km) long.

Before the Laerdal Tunnel (*below*) was built, the longest road tunnel in the world was the St. Gotthard Tunnel in Switzerland.

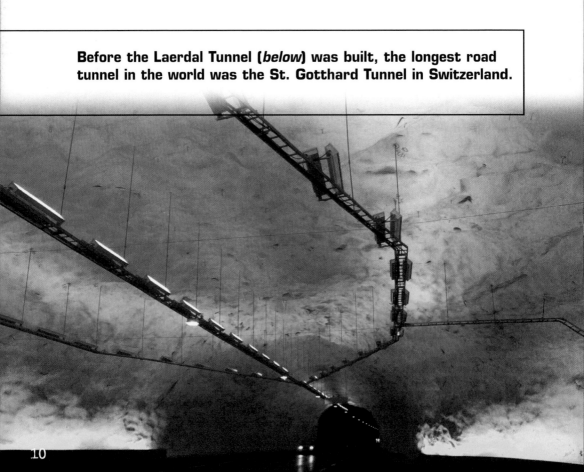

It connected to the middle of where the main tunnel would run. Workers coming through the access tunnel could dig from the middle of the tunnel toward each end, while other workers dug from the ends toward the middle. Digging from four directions made the tunneling go much faster. The access tunnel also gave workers a way to remove the rock and debris after each blast.

The Air Down There

The Laerdal Tunnel officially opened on November 27, 2000. The most amazing feature of the Laerdal Tunnel is its system for bringing fresh air into the tunnel. With a long tunnel, the air pollution produced by car and truck exhaust can reach dangerous levels. The Laerdal Tunnel is the first tunnel in world to have its own air treatment plant. It is located near the Aurland end of the tunnel.

Two giant fans are located near each end of the Laerdal Tunnel. They draw clean air into the tunnel. Then the dirty

Go Toward the Light

Driving through the Laerdal Tunnel takes about twenty minutes. Without the right design and lighting, this drive could be boring and possibly make drivers sleepy or nervous. To solve these problems, the Laerdal Tunnel is broken into four sections by three large caverns. Although the caverns are still completely enclosed, they are about three times wider than the rest of the tunnel. They provide space for emergency vehicles and for cars to turn around. One cavern is located more than 3 miles (5 km) from each end of the tunnel. The third cavern is located at the middle of the tunnel.

White light is used through the tunnel itself, while blue and yellow lights are used in the cavern openings. The lights make it look as if a driver is heading toward natural sunlight. Golden lights along the ground make the cavern look as it might during a sunrise. This change in the tunnel's lighting helps keep drivers calmer and more awake and aware of their surroundings.

Safety First

Fire is always a concern when building tunnels. The Laerdal Tunnel is one of the safest in the world. It has emergency phones every 820 feet (250 m). The phones are easily identified by the SOS on the outside. The phones have separate emergency channels to reach the police, ambulance, and fire departments.

Fire extinguishers are located every 410 feet (125 m) inside the tunnel. The Laerdal Tunnel also has fifteen emergency turn-around areas for large vehicles. Special wiring inside the tunnel allows people to use car radios and cell phones. Cameras at both entrances to the tunnel count and keep track of all traffic going in and out of the tunnel.

Emergency crews in the Mont Blanc Tunnel in France practice often to be prepared for real emergencies.

air is pushed out. It travels down a shaft, or tube, to the treatment plant. Pollutants are filtered out of the dirty air. Then clean air is sent back inside the tunnel. The Laerdal Tunnel is not only the longest road tunnel, it is also one of the cleanest.

MEGA FACTS

The first road tunnel in the world was the Holland Tunnel in New York. It was completed in 1927 and is more than 1 mile (1.6 km) long. The Hoosac Tunnel — a railroad tunnel in Massachusetts — was completed in 1875. It was the first tunnel to use a system to provide fresh air.

CHAPTER 3

INTO THE UNDERGROUND

Flowing between England and France, the English Channel separates the island nation of Britain from the rest of Europe. Throughout recorded history, the channel has been both a blessing and a problem. The rough waters provided England with protection against invasion. The dangerous channel, however, also slowed trade with other countries.

In 1984, British Prime Minister Margaret Thatcher and French President François Mitterand decided to fix the problem of slow trade between Britain and France. They announced a plan to build a massive tunnel under the English Channel. Officials of each country also agreed to turn construction of the tunnel into a friendly contest.

In 1987, construction on the Channel Tunnel began. Workers started digging in both England and France. They competed to see which country could reach the middle of the tunnel first. The Channel Tunnel is often called the Chunnel. It actually consists of three separate tunnels — two train tunnels and a service tunnel.

Shaking Hands With Fate

It took seven years for workers at each end of the Chunnel to inch their way toward each other. They used tunnel boring machines (TBMs) to slowly carve

THE CHUNNEL

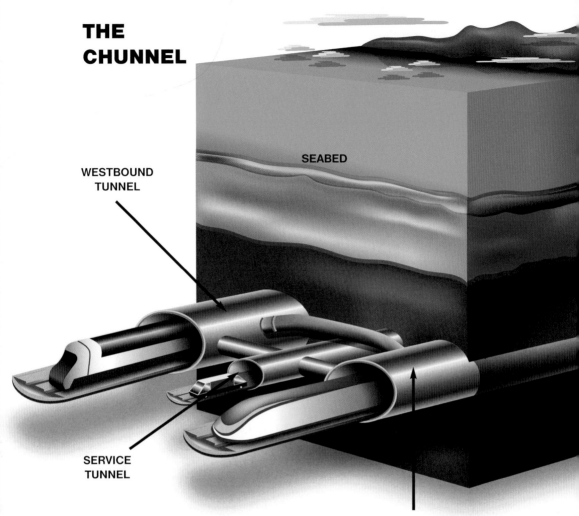

SEABED

WESTBOUND
TUNNEL

SERVICE
TUNNEL

EASTBOUND
TUNNEL

This diagram shows the Chunnel's
three tunnels. Each one is
connected to the others for easy
access for repairs and safety.

MEGA FACTS

In 1802, French ruler Napoleon
Bonaparte presented the idea of
an English Channel tunnel to officials in England.
The British were afraid France would invade
England, however, so they refused his plan.

through the soft earth. Following the machines were other workers who lined the tunnel surfaces with concrete. Workers in France and in England labored on all three tunnels at the same time. As workers guided the TBMs, engineers constantly checked their progress. The engineers had to make sure that when the two ends of the tunnel met, they would be lined up and could be perfectly joined together.

Engineers used a laser guidance system to keep the path straight. Each TBM was fitted with a laser on its drill head. A beam of light was bounced from the laser to a control panel in the tunnel. This system gave accurate readings about the TBM's course to engineers.

On December 1, 1990, workers drilled the final hole of the Chunnel. The English workers won the contest. They reached the middle of the tunnel before French workers. The contest did not seem to matter, however, as an English

The Weather Channel

Travel across the English Channel can be very dangerous. With bad weather often brewing above the channel's waterline, its waters can be extremely rough. Rainy, windy weather make boat travel difficult. Frequent, thick fog makes travel in the channel downright dangerous.

Other troubles lie below the water. Ridges of sand along the floor of the English Channel cause tricky, swift currents. These conditions above and below the water combine to make travel through the channel quite risky. Ocean experts have studied the weather in the channel for many years. They have discovered that there are only about sixty days during the year when the weather in the English Channel is clear for a full twenty-four hours.

Boring Tunnels

The ground under the English Channel posed a big problem to engineers. It was a soft mix of rock, chalk, and clay. An American company designed a special tunnel boring machine (TBM) for the Chunnel engineers.

The TBM was shaped like a giant can laid on its side. At one end was a rotating cutting head that measured 50 feet (15 m) across. Several TBMs were used to drill through the Channel floor. Some of them were as tall as a three-story building. Many TBMs were more than 8,000 feet (2,400 m) long. A single TBM weighed more than 15,000 tons (13,607 tonnes). Using TBMs, workers were able to move more than 750 feet (230 m) of chalk and rock each day. A total of eleven TBMs were used to dig the Channel Tunnel.

As the TBMs drilled, they left behind piles of crushed rock and other debris. Workers used conveyor belts to remove debris from the tunnel. More than 24,000 tons (21,772 tonnes) of debris was removed from the tunnel every hour.

Tunnel boring machines, like this one, make digging tunnels faster and safer than in years past.

worker and a French worker shook hands through the final hole. It was the first physical link between the two countries.

The Chunnel officially opened on May 6, 1994. When it was finished, the

Chunnel became the second longest rail tunnel in the world. It stretches 31 miles (50 km) between England and France. The Chunnel's underwater section of 24 miles (39 km), however, is the longest underwater section of tunnel in the world.

The Eurostar "bullet" trains travel about about **100** miles (**161** km) per hour through the Chunnel. They are capable, however, of speeds up to **186** miles (**300** km) per hour!

CHAPTER 4

BELOW ROUGH WATERS

The Seikan Tunnel in Japan is the longest rail tunnel in the world. The 33-mile (53-km) tunnel connects two islands of Japan. It links the large, main island of Honshu with the northern island of Hokkaido. It is also the deepest railway tunnel in the world. A 14-mile (23-km) section of the Seikan Tunnel runs underwater, beneath the Tsugaru Strait. At the tunnel's deepest point, it lies 788 feet (240 m) below the strait.

Planning for a connection between the Japanese islands began as early as the 1930s. The Tsugaru Strait is an extremely dangerous body of water. Before the tunnel's construction, the only way to get between Honshu and Hokkaido was by ferry. The boat ride was a treacherous trip. Giant storms, called typhoons, are common in that area.

Not So Solid Ground

The Seikan Tunnel had to be built in three parts. Workers needed a pilot tunnel, a service tunnel, and a main tunnel. The pilot tunnel allowed geologists to study the rock under the Tsugaru Strait. Construction of the pilot tunnel began in 1964. Geologists found that several fault lines ran through the ground under the strait. They also discovered the rock was too soft to use a TBM.

SEIKAN TUNNEL

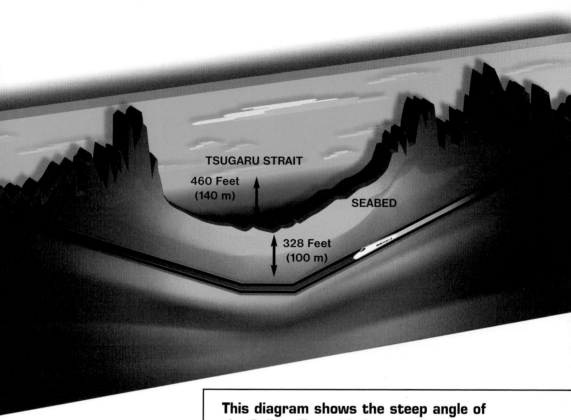

TSGARU STRAIT

460 Feet
(140 m)

SEABED

328 Feet
(100 m)

This diagram shows the steep angle of
the Seikan Tunnel below the Tsugaru
Strait. It is not only the longest rail
tunnel, but one of the world's deepest.

MEGA FACTS

Crossing the Tsugaru Strait was
also dangerous because of heavy
ship traffic. Ship crashes are very common
in the crowded strait.

Disaster Strikes

On September 26, 1954, a vicious typhoon ripped through the Tsugaru Strait. Winds reached more than 100 miles (161 km) per hour during the storm. Five ferries capsized in the high waves, killing more than 1,400 people. More than 1,100 people died on one ferry alone.

The Japanese people were angry. They pushed the Japanese government to find a better way to travel between the islands. Unfortunately, the weather also made building a bridge too risky. A tunnel was the only option. After the typhoon disaster, officials at the Japanese National Railways sped up plans for the Seikan Tunnel.

第4列車

MC-15

Construction of the main tunnel began in 1971. Workers used the old fashioned drill and blast method. They also used newer methods to stop the tunnel walls from collapsing. They injected the rock with thick grout to strengthen and waterproof the walls of the tunnel. Then workers built a steel frame around the walls of the tunnel. They sprayed a layer of reinforced concrete over the steel frame for extra support.

Workers used electric cars (*shown above*) to get from one place to another when building the Seikan Tunnel.

Flood in the Seikan

Building a tunnel under water is very dangerous. Water pressure around the tunnel brings the threat of flooding. In May 1976, the fear of a flood came true. Undiscovered weak spots in the rock caused a giant blowout in the Seikan Tunnel wall. Water rushed into the tunnel at 80 tons (73 tonnes) per minute! Workers had to shut down 2 miles (3 km) of the service tunnel and 1 mile (1.6 km) of the main tunnel.

Workers eventually controlled the flooding. It took them more than two months. They pumped water out of the tunnel. Then they rerouted the service tunnel to avoid the weakened areas of rock. Unbelievably, no workers died in the flood.

Marching to the Middle

Engineers made sure the workers digging from each end of the Seikan Tunnel joined up exactly in the middle. The engineers had to check measurements constantly. A tiny error on either side could put the entire

Seikan Tunnel off course. Despite slow and dangerous work conditions, the two ends of the main tunnel met on March 16, 1985. The project took more than twenty years from the date of the first blast in the pilot tunnel. Work was still far from finished, however.

Workers had to lay the railway tracks that would carry trains through the Seikan Tunnel. Rail service in the tunnel did not begin until 1988. Engineers originally designed the Seikan Tunnel for super-fast bullet trains. The enormous cost of the project, however, prevented them from being used. The original price tag for the tunnel in 1971 was $783 million. By the time construction had been completed, the tunnel had cost more than $6 billion!

Many in Japan fear the tunnel may never earn back its steep costs. The cost of tunnel repairs continue to add to its already high price tag, while air travel competes with the rail tunnel for passengers. The fate of the world's longest tunnel remains to be seen.

MEGA FACTS

More than 280,000 tons (254,011 tonnes) of explosives were used to blast away rock during construction of the Seikan Tunnel.

CHAPTER 5

LONGEST OF ALL

The longest tunnels in the world do not carry cars, trains, or even people. These super-long tunnels are part of a system called an aqueduct. They help bring fresh water from a river, lake, or reservoir to a city or town. Most aqueducts are a combination of bridges, canals, and long tunnels.

The Delaware Aqueduct tunnel is the longest continuous rock tunnel in the world. Construction of the Delaware Aqueduct began in 1937. This solid rock tunnel was completed in 1944. Originally 84 miles (135 km) long, the Delaware Aqueduct tunnel stretches from the Catskill Mountains to New York City. It runs under the Hudson River and into the Bronx, one of the city's five sections called boroughs. In 1965, the tunnel was expanded to its current length of 105 miles (169 km).

Blasted by Sandhogs

The New York system of aqueducts is an enormous maze of tunnels. One of the newest tunnels is City Tunnel No. 3. Construction on the tunnel began in 1970. When it is finished in 2020, City Tunnel No. 3 will be 60 miles (97 km) long.

City workers, known as "sandhogs," used the drill and blast method to start digging City Tunnel No. 3.

Robots in the Aqueduct

The Delaware Aqueduct carries half of New York City's daily water supply. More than 50 million gallons (190 million liters) of water travel through the tunnel each day. In recent years, the 13-foot- (4-m-) wide, concrete-lined tunnel has begun to leak. Between 10 million gallons (38 million l) and 36 million gallons (136 million l) of water may have seeped out of the tunnel each day for the past five years.

Beginning in 2001, workers began inspecting the tunnel using submersible vehicles. These remote-controlled robots traveled 45 miles (72 km) through the Delaware Aqueduct tunnel. Some leaks have been found and repairs have been made. City workers still have much of the aqueduct left to fix, however, before all the leaks can be stopped.

Anywhere from one to three explosions were set off each day. After each blast, workers removed the muck, or debris, from the tunnel on conveyor belts. More than 1,500 tons (1,360 tonnes) of debris are removed from City Tunnel No. 3 each day.

After the initial dig, workers on City Tunnel No. 3 started using TBMs. They are some of the same TBMs used to dig the Chunnel under the English Channel. The TBMs have allowed workers to push forward through almost 75 feet (23 m) of rock each day. Workers can move much faster using TBMs instead of the drill and blast method. Once the sections of tunnel are carved by the TBMs, workers line the tunnel walls with concrete for added strength.

MEGA FACTS

The most famous part of the Delaware Aqueduct is not its long tunnel. John Roebling designed the bridge portion of the aqueduct. He is the same architect who designed the Brooklyn Bridge.

No one walking or driving on New York City streets has a clue that giant metal grinding machines are at work beneath their feet. TBMs do not create vibrations or noises that travel up to street level. When City Tunnel

Enormous tunnel drills carve holes in rock so workers can place explosives inside.

Gravitational Pull

The second longest continuous rock tunnel in the world is the Päijänne Water Tunnel in Finland. Like the Delaware Aqueduct, it is carved out of solid bedrock. The 75-mile- (120-km-) long tunnel was built from 1972 to 1982. Workers carved the tunnel using powerful drills and blasting techniques.

Like most aqueducts, the Päijänne Water Tunnel relies on gravity to move the water forward. From its beginning to its end, the slope, or angle, of the tunnel drops 118 feet (36 m). Much of the water from the tunnel is pure and clean even before going through the water treatment plant.

No. 3 is completed, it can carry water that currently runs through City Tunnels No. 1 and 2. Officials can then find and repair leaks in those tunnels while maintaining the supply of water needed by New Yorkers.

This maintenance engineer is just one of the thousands of workers involved in the construction of New York's City Water Tunnel No. 3.

MEGA FACTS

The muck taken from City Tunnel No. 3 could fill a football field with a giant pile of crushed rock more than 250 feet (76 m) high.

1802 Napoleon Bonaparte presents idea for a tunnel under the English Channel to English officials. England rejects the idea.

1825 Sir Marc Brunel invents the tunneling shield.

1875 Hoosac Tunnel completed in Massachusetts.

1927 Holland Tunnel completed in New York.

1944 Delaware Aqueduct tunnel is completed at 84 miles (135 km) long.

1954 Typhoon disaster in Japan sinks five ferries. More than 1,400 people die.

1965 Delaware Aqueduct tunnel is lengthened to 105 miles (169 km).

1970 Construction of New York's City Tunnel No. 3 begins.

1982 Päijänne Water Tunnel completed in Finland. It is 75 miles (120 km) long.

1988 Seikan Tunnel opens and becomes the longest rail tunnel at 33 miles (53 km) long.

1994 The Chunnel officially opens. With a length of 31 miles (50 km), it is the second longest rail tunnel.

2000 Laerdal Tunnel opens for traffic. Fifteen miles (24 km) long, it is the longest road tunnel.

2001 Underwater submersible inspects Delaware Aqueduct tunnel for leaks.

The Ted Williams Tunnel runs under Boston Harbor in the city of Boston. Opened in 1995, it is part of a tunnel construction project nicknamed the "Big Dig." It is the most expensive highway project in U.S. history.

GLOSSARY

aqueduct – man-made system of bridges, canals, and tunnels to transport water

capsized – flipped over

conveyor belts – endless moving mechanical belts used for moving materials from place to place

detonated – set off explosives

drill and blast method – tunneling method in which holes are drilled, then packed with explosives that are used to blow apart rock

engineers – people who use scientific knowledge to design and build bridges, roads, tunnels, and buildings

fault lines – breaks in a mass of rock caused by shifting of Earth's crust. Faults are the source of many earthquakes.

ferry – a large boat used to transport people or automobiles across water

geologist – a person who studies the rock layers of Earth

grout – a substance used to fill cracks and crevasses in rock or masonry

hydraulic – powered by liquids put under high pressure

laser – a device that sends out a very narrow and powerful beam of light

muck – crushed rock and other debris removed from a tunnel

reinforced concrete – concrete with steel bars or mesh added to it for extra support

reservoir – place where water is collected and stored for use

tunneling shield – a structure used for support when tunneling through the very soft ground under a waterway. The shield keeps the tunnel from collapsing while being dug.

typhoons – severe tropical hurricanes occurring in the western Pacific Ocean

Books

The Chunnel. Building World Landmarks (series). Joanne Mattern (Blackbirch Press)

The Chunnel: The Building of a 200-Year-Old Dream. High Interest Books (series). Jil Fine (Children's Press)

The Longest Tunnel. Extreme Places (series). Kelly Borchelt (Kidhaven Press)

Tunnels. Building Amazing Structures (series). Chris Oxlade (Heinemann Library)

Video

Building Big: Tunnels (WGBH Boston Video) NR

Web Sites

Building Big: All About Tunnels
www.pbs.org/wgbh/buildingbig/tunnel/index.html
Information on tunnels and the materials and methods used to build them

World's Longest Tunnels
home.no.net/lotsberg
Lists of the longest tunnels and links to tunnel sites

Publisher's note to educators and parents: Our editors have carefully reviewed these Web sites to ensure that they are suitable for children. Many Web sites change frequently, however, and we cannot guarantee that a site's future contents will continue to meet our high standards of quality and educational value. Be advised that children should be closely supervised whenever they access the Internet.

INDEX

About the Author

Susan K. Mitchell is a teacher and the author of several children's picture books. Susan has also written many non-fiction chapter books for kids. She lives near Houston, Texas, with her husband, two daughters, a dog, and two cats. She dedicates this book to her sister, Lorie.